Left-handed crochet

Regina Hurlburt

Drawings by Prue Bucknall

VAN NOSTRAND REINHOLD COMPANY
NEW YORK   CINCINNATI   TORONTO   LONDON   MELBOURNE

By the same author:
Left-handed Needlepoint
Left-handed Knitting

Copyright © 1979 by Regina Hurlburt
Library of Congress Catalog Card Number 78-17162
ISBN 0-442-23590-9

Printed in the U.S.A.

Published in 1979 by Van Nostrand Reinhold Company
A division of Litton Educational Publishing, Inc.
135 West 50th Street, New York, NY 10020, U.S.A.

Van Nostrand Reinhold Limited
1410 Birchmount Road
Scarborough, Ontario M1P 2E7, Canada

Van Nostrand Reinhold Australia Pty. Ltd.
17 Queen Street
Mitcham, Victoria 3132, Australia

Van Nostrand Reinhold Company Limited
Molly Millars Lane
Wokingham, Berkshire, England

16 15 14 13 12 11 10 9 8 7 6 5 4 3 2

Library of Congress Cataloging in Publication Data

Hurlburt, Regina.
  Left-handed crochet.

  1. Crocheting. I. Title.
TT820.H86   746.4'34   78-17162
ISBN 0-442-23590-9

Foreword

This book, like my books on needlepoint and knitting, grows out of my continual wandering through the Victoria and Albert Museum as well as the new London Museum. These museums are affectionately known as the "Attics of Britain." Any fabric, handcraft samples, books, or patterns referring to handcrafts from the past 200 years can usually be found there.

These wanderings made me realize that the crafts of knitting and crochet have run parallel and have crossed each other through the centuries; today they are so closely allied that some of the same stitches can be created by either method.

Having mastered knitting with the left hand, I continued on to crochet, again devising my own left-handed ways. I hope that you will have as much pleasure as I have had.

Contents

Crochet history

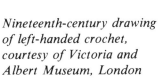

Nineteenth-century drawing of left-handed crochet, courtesy of Victoria and Albert Museum, London

Fine crochet developed from a type of embroidery originally called *tambouring*, which was used for decorative purposes and for ornamenting the surfaces of fabric. By the end of the eighteenth century, the French had derived a decorative version of tambouring that they called *crochet*. It took its name from the French word for *hook* rather than the word for the frame, *tambour*, since crochet does not require a frame. As evolved, crochet was no longer a surface decoration, but was instead an independent weaving of a single thread that had a lacelike appearance and was still used for decorative purposes.

At the same time, wool crochet was developing in the northern parts of the world primarily as a method of producing warm garments. It was regarded as another form of knitting. The stitch that best illustrates the alliance between knitting and crochet is called the Afghan or Tunisian crochet.

The crochet hook used in this stitch is large and, like

a knitting needle, is of uniform thickness and has a knob at one end to keep the stitches from slipping off.

Crochet took on a renewed popularity after World War II when increasing numbers of women realized that it could be utilized for garment making. In the past twenty-five years crochet patterns have been refined and stitches and techniques advanced so that high-fashion garments are at the fingertips of everyone willing to try, whether they be left-handed or otherwise.

Left-handed crochet

Crochet, like knitting, is a craft that creates a fabric from a single thread; unlike knitting, it uses a hook as the instrument of weaving.

Crochet uses the starting loop to build a length of chain. The weaver then works back over the length of the chain and completes each stitch until a single loop is again left on the hook before the next stitch is begun. This loop remains as a working loop throughout all the crochet, beginning with the slip loop. It is not removed until the section of fabric is completed and ready to be fastened off.

Yarns

Any yarn can be used to crochet as long as the correct sized hook is used with it. This will cover a wide range of wools, cottons, and synthetics. Interesting effects have been achieved with ribbon, sisal, and even leather strips.

If you are just beginning to learn the craft of crochet it is wise to purchase the yarns recommended in the patterns. The designer of the pattern has carefully worked out the yarn weight in combination with the recommended hook to arrive at the number of stitches to the inch or centimeter that will result in the correct size and shape of the finished garment.

Choose your yarn with some care. Part of the pleasure of crochet lies in handling a yarn that feels good in your hands. If the yarn does not please you, change your pattern before you change the yarn prescribed in the pattern, unless you are an expert. Many people leave work incomplete when they have chosen working materials they are not really happy with.

Purchase all your yarn at the same time. Dye lots vary, and there is nothing more frustrating than to be short a skein or ball of yarn to complete your work. It is unlikely that you will be able to find a skein from the same dye lot at a later date. In fact, it is wise to buy a bit more than the recommended amount. You may need it for your 4-inch (10 cm) testing squares, or you may find that you work more tightly than the recommended tension in the pattern and therefore will need more yarn then is called for. Check the dye lot numbers of all the balls or skeins carefully to be certain that the numbers are all the same, before you leave the shop.

Yarns used for crochet may be either thick or fine. When the yarn description uses the word *ply* it refers to the number of single threads twisted together to produce a specific yarn. The thickness of thread may vary from one spinning mill to the next so 3 ply of one mill may be thicker than that of another mill. Wool or a combination of wool and synthetic is still the most popular yarn. Wool gives a yarn flexibility, and synthetic fibers give it improved strength as well as quick-drying properties. It is much simpler to block and shape natural yarns with a bit of Orlon or nylon added than it is to block pure synthetic yarns. This

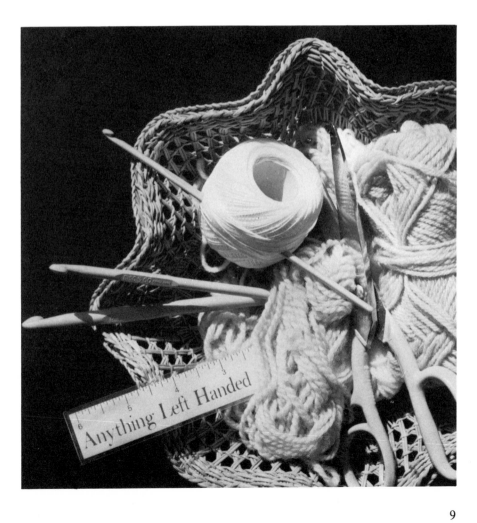

becomes important since the blocking and shaping process may be necessary to correct uneven work.

Advances in the design of crochet stitches have brought about the wider use of Aran type yarns for crochet. You can now create an Aran sweater without ever touching a knitting needle.

Cotton, like wool, comes in various weights and thicknesses. Thin thread is used for lace-making or decorative crochet. Thick rug yarn is used for garments, bed covers, or even rugs. You will find that cotton yarn is also frequently spun in combination with acrylic or linen for greater strength.

There is a wide variety of novelty yarns available for crochet. They range from lamé thread to ribbon or straw, proving the great flexibility of the craft and its uses. All you need to be certain of is that the hook you use is the proper size for the yarn.

Until worldwide weights and measures are standardized, the yarn buyer may experience some confusion when confronted with a skein of yarn made in Europe and labelled with a metric weight for use in a pattern designed in the United States with a yarn quantity recommendation in ounces. The chart below should serve as a guide when buying yarn.

Ounce to gram	Gram to ounce
1 oz. = 28.35 g 4 oz. = 113.4 g 8 oz. = 226.8 g 1 lb. = 454 g	25 g = 7/8 oz. 50 g = 1 3/4 oz. 1 kg/1000 g = 2 lbs. 2 oz.

If your pattern calls for ounces of yarn and the yarn manufacturer has weighed the yarn by the metric system, you will have to buy it in 25-gram ball units. Remember that 1 ounce is slightly *more* than 25 grams, so be certain to increase the number of balls you purchase. For example, if the pattern calls for ten 1-ounce balls, you will need twelve 25-gram balls.

The wrapper bands around the balls or skeins are marked to give you information on the composition of the yarn as well as the washing instructions. It is a good idea to use soap or detergent manufactured specifically for knitwear. It is meant to dissolve easily in tepid water and usually does not contain bleach. Never soak knitted or crocheted items; it is wiser to wash them immediately.

Hooks

The better crochet hooks, like the better knitting needles, are made of steel or aluminum. The best are light-weight aluminum with a thin plastic coating. The steel hooks are used mainly with fine wool yarn, fine cotton thread, or linen thread. Aluminum hooks are used predominantly with wool, heavy or coarse cotton, and synthetic yarns.

The higher the number the greater the diameter of the hook.

Since crochet hooks hold no stitches except for the working loop, they are made in one easy-to-handle length no matter what the diameter. An exception is the Afghan or Tunisian crochet hook, which has the look of a knitting needle with a crochet hook at one end and a knitting needle stop at the other end. The method of working this stitch requires a number of stitches to be held on the hook; hooks are available in various lengths.

It is false economy to use warped or rough hooks. They may cause your tension to become distorted. The cheap plastic variety warp easily and frequently have too sharp a hook, which may split the yarn. Take good care of your crochet hooks, keep them in their sheath, and they will give you many years of good service.

American	International Size Range of Hooks (metric)
K/10½	7
J/10	6
I/9	5.5
H/8	5
G/6	4.5
F/5	4
E/4	3.5
D/3	
C/2	3
B/1	2.5

Having purchased your pattern, yarn or cotton thread, and hooks, there are several other useful items to add to your work bag or box. It is much pleasanter to have all your working items in one place as it is simpler to then pick up and begin work in any spare moments.

A 12-inch (30.5 cm) ruler for measuring your work. This ruler is also useful for measuring the number of stitches to the inch or centimeter on your practice squares.

A strong, unstretchable tape measure for measuring yourself or the person for whom the piece is intended.

Stainless steel pins for blocking and pressing your work.

Blunt-tipped wool or tapestry needles for stitching together sections of the work.

A small, sharp pair of scissors for snipping threads or bits of yarn.

A small note pad and pencil to keep a record of your work. This is a very handy item to always have in your work bag or box; it is so much easier to have a written record of the rows of crochet worked, rather than having to recount every time you pick up your work.

A plastic bag to keep your work clean. Don't allow your efforts to become grimy.

Tension

Correct tension is the key to the successful working of a crochet design; it means that you have achieved the same number of stitches and rows to the inch or centimeter as the designer intended.

When you first learn to crochet it is most important to keep practicing with a 4-inch (10 cm) square. This will help you to learn your own way of working. If your habit is to work tightly, then you may have too many stitches to the inch (cm). You must then change to a larger size hook. If you work loosely, you will have insufficient stitches to the inch (cm), and will have to change to a smaller size hook.

Whether you are a beginner or a more experienced crocheter, you really should make a tension sample whenever you begin a new design or stitch. The designer may have a tendency to work either more loosely or more tightly than you do, so simply assuming that your tension is average and that it is therefore not necessary to check against pattern instructions may result in a size of the finished work that is not quite what it should be. All measurements and sizes are based on the specific designer's individual way of working, and that, of course, will vary.

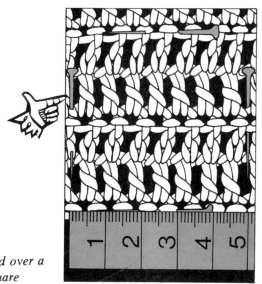

Tension measured over a
2-inch (5 cm) square

After you have completed your tension sample, pin it down on a flat surface. Be certain not to stretch it. Use your 12-inch (30.5 cm) measure and mark with straight pins a 2-inch (5 cm) area. Count the number of stitches between the pins as well as the number of rows. They should agree with the tension requirements of your pattern.

Turning chains and stitch abbreviations

Of equal importance to learning the basic crochet stitches is understanding the use of the turning chain. The chain is used because in crochet, unlike knitting, it is necessary to add extra chains at the beginning of each row to bring the hook up to the level of the stitch being created. When studying a new pattern check carefully whether the turning chain instructions are given at the beginning or at the end of the row. Instructions may vary from pattern to pattern but the important principle to keep in mind is that the turning chain is, in effect, the *first* stitch at the *beginning* of every row. To allow for this, the first stitch of each row must be skipped and the actual pattern stitch worked into the second stitch of the previous row. At the end of the row the last stitch is worked into the turning chain of the previous row. This is the general rule for row or round crochet unless your pattern states differently.

Listed here are the abbreviations for the basic stitches, turning chains required for each stitch, and British equivalent names for the same stitches.

	American			British	
ch	chain			chain	ch
ss or sl st	slip stitch			slip stitch	ss
sc	single crochet	chain 1		double crochet	dc
hdc	half double crochet	chain 2		half treble	htr
dc	double crochet	chain 3		treble	tr
tr	triple crochet	chain 4		double treble	dtr
dtr	double triple	chain 5		triple treble	tr tr
tr tr	triple triple	chain 6		quad treble	qd tr

General abbreviations

alt	alternate(ly)
approx	approximate(ly)
beg	begin(ning)
cl	cluster
cm	centimeter(s)
cont	continue
dec	decrease
foll	follow(ing)
gr	group
g	gram(s)
in	inch(es)
inc	increase

ISR	International Size Range of hooks
lp(s)	loop(s)
No	number
patt	pattern
rem	remain(ing)
rep	repeat
rnd	round
RS	right side of work
sk	skip
sl st	slip stitch in seaming
st(s)	stitch(es)
tog	together
WS	wrong side of work
yrh	yarn round hook ⎫ both mean the same
yo	yarn over hook ⎭

An asterisk, *, in a pattern row denotes that the stitches after this sign must be repeated from that point to the end of the row or to the last number of stitches given. In general, an instruction shown in parentheses, ( ), means that this section of the pattern is to be worked for all sizes. Instructions shown in square brackets, [], denote larger sizes. This does vary, however, so when studying your pattern, make certain that it is clear which set of brackets are for which instructions.

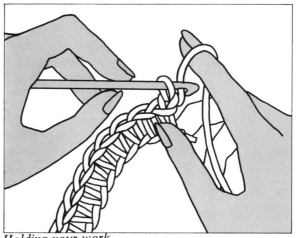

Holding your work

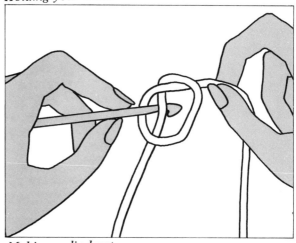

Making a slip knot

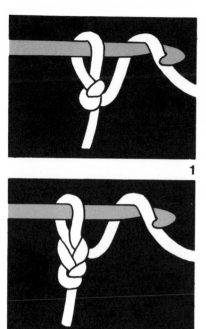

*Three stages in
creating a chain*

Chain stitch

Crochet begins with making a length of chains that form the foundation row. The first step is to make a slip knot. Tighten the loop gently so that the hook will still be free to pass through easily. Hold the hook with the slip knot in your left hand and guide the yarn with your right hand. Pass the hook under and then over the yarn in your right hand, thus catching the yarn with the hook. Holding the bottom of the slip knot with your right hand, draw the yarn through the slip knot on the hook from back to front. You have now made the first chain and have a working loop on your hook. Repeat this working method until you have the required number of chains. As you are working the chain stitch move your thumb and forefinger up the chain, holding it with just enough tension to keep it firm for the hook to pass through, but not too tightly or it will stretch your yarn. Allow the yarn to run freely over the fingers of your right hand.

Slip stitch

This stitch is rarely used to form a pattern as it is the shallowest of the crochet stitches. It is used as a link between the last stitch and the first stitch to form a round or to maneuver from one position to another along a row when shaping is necessary. Insert the crochet hook from front to back under both loops at the top of a stitch, catch the yarn around the hook and pull it through the two top loops as well as the working loop on the hook. You have now worked one slip stitch and are left with a working loop on your hook.

Some pattern instructions may require the slip

Working a slip stitch

stitch to be worked into the beginning chain stitches to give added strength and an even finish to the chain before the pattern stitch begins. To do this, use the same method, but pick up a single loop of your chain rather then the double loops.

Single crochet

Single crochet is the shortest and, therefore, the tightest stitch. Chain the required number of chains, plus 1 extra. For example, make 13 chains for 12 single crochet stitches.

1st row Insert the hook from front to back into the 3rd chain from the hook. *Wind yarn round hook and draw a loop through. This will give you 2 loops on the hook. Wind yarn round hook again and draw through both loops on the hook. You have now made 1 single crochet, and you have a working loop remaining on the hook. The 2 missed chains at the beginning count as your first stitch. Insert hook into next chain. Repeat from * into each chain until you reach the end of the row.

2nd row Turn the work and make a single chain to serve as a turning chain. Skip the turning chain and first single crochet and insert the hook under the double loop at the top of the next single crochet. Yarn round hook and continue as instructed for previous row.

These 2 rows will form your pattern.

3

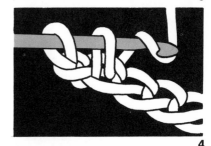

1

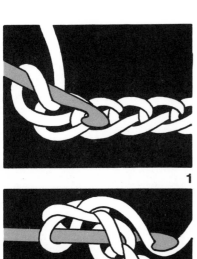

2

*Five steps in working
the single crochet*

4

5

Three steps in half double crochet

1

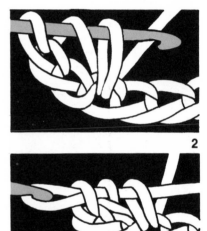

2

3

Half double crochet

Crochet required number of chains as for the single crochet.

1st row   Yarn round hook and insert hook into the 3rd chain from the hook. * Yarn round hook and draw a loop through. This will give you 3 loops on the hook. Yarn round hook and draw yarn through all 3 loops on the hook. Yarn round hook and insert hook into next chain. Repeat from * until all the chains have been worked.

2nd row   Turn and make 2 turning chains. Skip the first half double crochet in the previous row and crochet as instructed for the 1st row.

These 2 rows make the half double crochet pattern.

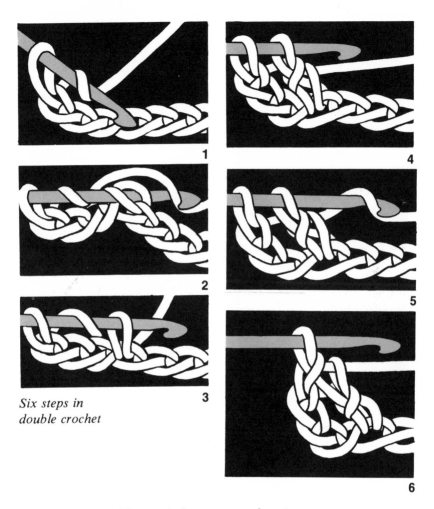

1

4

2

5

3

6

*Six steps in
double crochet*

Double crochet

Crochet the required number of chains plus 2 extra
chains; for example, 14 chains for 12 double crochet
stitches.

1st row Yarn round hook and insert into 4th chain
from the hook. * Yarn round hook again and draw a
loop through. You will have 3 loops on your hook.
Yarn round hook and draw through 2 of the loops on

the hook. You are now left with 2 loops on the hook. Yarn round hook again and draw through the 2 remaining loops on the hook. Yarn round hook and insert hook into next chain. Repeat from * for the balance of the row. The 3 missed chains at the beginning of the row count as your first stitch.

2nd row   Work 3 turning chains. Skip the first double crochet. Yarn round hook and insert under both loops at the top of the next double crochet and continue as instructed in the previous row.

These 2 rows make the double crochet pattern.

Triple crochet

Make a chain of 15 stitches—12 stitches plus 3 extra chains.

1st row   Yarn round hook twice, insert the hook into the 5th chain from the hook. *Yarn round hook again and draw a loop through, giving you 4 loops on the hook. Yarn round hook and draw through 2 loops on the hook, leaving you with 3 loops on the hook. Yarn round hook and draw through 2 loops again. Yarn round hook and draw through the 2 remaining loops. You now have a triple crochet with the 4 missing chains counting as the 1st stitch. Yarn round hook twice and insert hook into next chain. Repeat from * until the end.

2nd row   Turn your work and chain 4 to serve as the turning chain. The turning chain will count as your 1st triple crochet. Skip the next triple crochet. Yarn round

Three steps in triple crochet

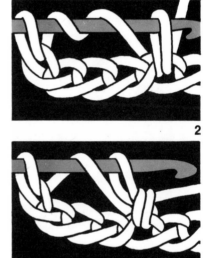

hook twice and insert hook into top loops of the next triple crochet stitch. Repeat instructions as given in 1st row.

The next two stitches are not used as frequently as the previous ones, but it is helpful to know about them should they ever occur in any of your patterns.

Drawing of
double triple crochet

Drawing of
triple triple crochet

Double triple crochet

Add 5 chains to your basic 10 chains, for a total of 15 chains.

1st row   Yarn round hook 3 times and insert hook into the 6th chain from the hook. Yarn round hook and draw through the top loops, giving you 5 loops on the hook. Yarn round hook and draw through 2 loops. Repeat this action 3 times until a single working loop remains on your hook. Continue across row, working every chain in this way.

2nd row   The turning chain for this stitch is 5 chains. Turn and wind yarn round hook as required and insert hook into the 2nd stitch of the previous row, continue as instructed for the 1st row.

Triple triple crochet

This is achieved simply by adding 6 chains to the basic 10 chains and one additional yarn round hook to the number in the previous stitch (4 yarn round hook) and then inserting through the 7th chain. Yarn round hook again and draw through the chain, giving you 6 loops. Continue with 1 yarn round the hook and draw through 2 loops at a time. This action is repeated 4 times until you remain with a single working loop on the hook. Work each chain in this way. At the end of the row turn, chain 6 turning chains. Begin repeating the stitches as in the 1st row and insert hook into 2nd stitch from the hook.

Afghan or Tunisian stitch

This interesting stitch or technique serves as a link between knitting and crochet. It is worked on a single hooked needle with a knob at one end similar to a knitting needle. Since all your loops remain on the hooked needle at every other row, always choose one of comfortable length to hold all the loops. This technique will give you a strong, firm fabric, and the charm of it is that, depending on the variations of stitches, the finished texture can resemble either crochet or knitting.

The first row is worked from left to right into each chain. The 2nd row is the completion of the first row, as you work back again from right to left. You will always have the right side of the crochet fabric facing you.

Begin as you would for regular crochet. Chain the required number of loops plus a working loop. You will not need extra chains to count as turning chains. In effect, 10 chains plus a working chain will give you 10 stitches.

1st row Insert hook into 2nd chain from hook, picking up just one of the top loops. Yarn round hook and draw a loop through the chain. Keep this loop on the hook. *Insert hook into next single top loop, yarn round hook and draw through the chain again. Again, keep this loop on the hook. Continue from * to the end of the row. The number of loops on the hook should be

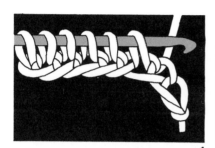

Basic Afghan stitch

1

2

3

*Three steps in Afghan
or Tunisian crochet*

Afghan double crochet

the same as the beginning chain. As you will see there is no need to turn.

2nd row   Work from right to left. Yarn round hook and draw a loop through the first loop on the hook, *yarn round hook and draw through 2 loops on hook. Repeat from * to end. Do not turn work. Working loop only will remain on hook.

3rd row   Work from left to right. Skip the first vertical loop at the front and *insert the hook from left to right behind the next vertical bar, yarn round hook and draw a loop through. Keep this loop on the hook and repeat from * to the end. No need to turn.

4th row   Repeat the 2nd row.

The 3rd and 4th row form the pattern for the basic Afghan Stitch. You must always end with the 4th row. It is wise to check the number of stitches on the hook at the end of every 3rd row as you may sometimes miss the last stitch when crocheting this row.

Afghan stocking stitch

Afghan double crochet   Crochet a length of chain giving you the exact number of stitches necessary.

1st row   Working from left to right, yrh, insert the hook into the 2nd ch from the hook, yrh and draw a loop through ch, yrh and draw through 2 loops on hook; * yrh, insert hook into next ch, yrh and draw loop through, yrh and draw through 2 loops on hook, rep from * to end. Do not turn. Check the number of loops on the hook. There should be the same amount as your beginning ch.

2nd row   Working from right to left, crochet as the 2nd row of basic Afghan stitch.

3rd row   Again working from left to right, 1ch to count as first stitch, skip first vertical loop at the front of the fabric, * yrh, insert hook from left to right behind next vertical loop of next stitch, yrh and draw a loop through, yrh and draw through the 2 loops on hook, rep from * to end. Do not turn.

4th row   Rep as 2nd row.

The 3rd and 4th row form the pattern. Always end with the 4th row.

Afghan stocking stitch   Make a length of chain as needed. Work first and 2nd row as given for basic Afghan stitch.

3rd row   Working from left to right, * insert hook from front to back between the next 2 vertical loops and below the top edge of the next st of the previous row, yrh, draw a loop through loosely, rep from * to end. Do not turn.

4th row   Rep 2nd row.

The 3rd and 4th row form the pattern. Always end with the 4th row.

Working in rounds

Working in rounds can produce flat fabrics as well as tubular seamless fabrics. This method means that the last stitch of each round is joined to the first stitch as you crochet around and around. There is no need to turn at the end as there is when working in flat rows. The right side of the fabric will always be facing you.

If you are crocheting a sweater in any of the basic stitches and wish it to be seamless in the body, keep in mind that the work will have to be divided to form armholes. Therefore, the tubular fabric will have to be turned so that the alternating rows are worked on the wrong side. The reason for this is that even the basic stitches will have a different appearance when worked

Two steps in forming a ring **1**

2

Crocheting a round into a ring

in the round.

Begin with a chain the exact length of the circumference needed. There is no need to make any extra turning chains. The last chain is joined to the first chain by a slip stitch to form a circle. Make certain that the chain is not twisted before you slip stitch to create the circle.

For a fabric that will always have the right side facing you, * work the necessary turning chains to form the 1st stitch and skip the 1st chain. Continue working 1 stitch into each chain to the end. Using a slip stitch, join the last stitch to the last chain of the turning chain, and continue from * for the required number of rows. It is helpful to use a bit of different colored thread to mark the beginning of the row.

If you are working a tubular fabric that requires alternate turning to the wrong side, begin with the same method of making chains and a joining slip stitch. Work the first round as in the previous instructions. After the joining of the last stitch to the first one with the slip stitch, turn the work so that the wrong side is facing you. The last stitch of the previous row now becomes the first stitch. Make the necessary number of turning chains for your stitch, skip the first stitch, and continue with your pattern stitch to the end of the round. Join with a slip stitch and continue in this manner for the required number of rounds until the fabric is to be divided. Then continue working in rows without joining.

To crochet flat fabrics in the round you must begin with a small number of stitches that are increased every round until the necessary size is reached. This can be done by means of additional stitches or chain spaces. A circular round is formed by the creation of 4 or multiples of 4, connecting the first stitch to the last stitch by a slip stitch.

Into this circle work in your pattern twice the number stitches used to make the chain, beginning by crocheting the necessary number of chains to form the first stitch of your pattern, then continuing the pattern stitch into the circle. Join the last stitch to the top of the turning chain with a slip stitch. In the next round, work the turning chain to count as the 1st stitch, and then work 1 stitch into the same place as the base of the turning chain. Continue by working 2 stitches into the

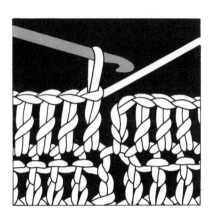

*To work tubular fabric
turning each round*

top of each stitch of the previous row. This will bring
the number of stitches to 4 times the original number
in your chain. Join again by a slip stitch into the top of
the turning chain.

In each of the following rounds increase by double
the number of stitches in original chain, i.e. 4 chains,
increase 8 stitches; 8 chains, increase 16 stitches.
Increase into the 1st and every other stitch of the next
round. Then into the 1st and every 3rd stitch in the
next round, and the 1st and every 4th stitch in the
round after that. Continue in this way depending on
how large a round you wish.

Increasing

If your pattern tells you to "increase 1 stitch at the beginning and the end of the next row," simply work the necessary number of turning chains at the beginning of the row and, instead of skipping the 1st stitch, work into it to increase the 1 stitch. Continue with your pattern across the row until 2 stitches remain. Crochet 2 stitches into the next stitch and work your final stitch into the turning chain of the previous row.

Increasing a stitch in the middle of a row is simple. Work your pattern until you reach the position that requires the increase, then work 2 stitches into the stitch instead of 1 and continue the pattern. It is wise to mark the position of the increase with a colored thread as the pattern may require that you increase 1 stitch on alternate rows or at given intervals. Alternating the position of subsequent increases with the first increase into the 1st stitch and the next increase into the 2nd stitch will give you a straight line increase. Using your pad and pencil to keep notes of these rows will save time.

To increase several stitches at the beginning of a row, begin by continuing with a series of chain stitches as you finish the previous row. If, for example, your instructions require an increase of 6 extra stitches while working in double crochet, make 5 extra chains plus 3 turning chains. This will give you a total of 8 chains. Work the next double crochet for the new row

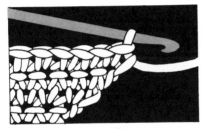

*Increasing one stitch at
either end of a row*

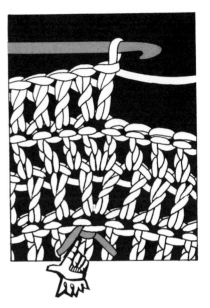

*Increasing a stitch in
the middle of a row*

*Increasing several stitches
at the beginning of a row*

First method of increasing several stitches at the end of a row

Second method of increasing several stitches at the end of a row

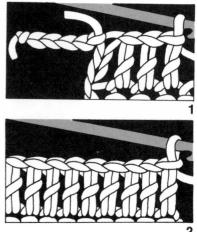

into the 5th chain from the hook. Continue working double crochet into each of the next 4 chains. This will create your 6 extra stitches. Continue working in pattern.

Increasing several stitches at the end of a row may be done by either of two methods.

The first, and possibly the best, method must be planned two rows before you come to the row in which the increase is to take place. For example, 2 rows before the row that is to be increased for a 6-stitch increase in double crochet, continue with a chain of 10 stitches. Skip the 1st chain and slip stitch into each of the next 6 chains, leaving the final 3 chains for the double crochet turning chain. You will find yourself with a bit of crochet looking like a mouse tail. This is the basis of your 6-stitch increase. Continue in pattern for 2 rows. The 2nd row will bring you back to the position for beginning your actual increase.

The second method my be considered simpler. Before working in pattern from left to right across the fabric to bring you to the point of increase, make a separate chain for the required number of stitches to be increased. Join this chain to the last stitch at the right end of your work by means of a slip stitch. Fasten off and break off the yarn. The bit of yarn left hanging can be woven in at the end of the section of fabric. Now work the pattern from left to right across the fabric. When you reach the bit of chain that you fastened on, work 1 stitch into each of the chains.

Decreasing

Decreasing, unlike increasing, requires a somewhat different method for each of the basic stitches.

To decrease 1 single crochet at each end of a row: Make 1 turning chain and skip the 1st single crochet. Insert hook into the next stitch and draw a loop through, then insert hook into the next stitch and draw a loop through. You will now have 3 loops on the hook. Yarn round hook and draw through all the loops on the hook. Continue in pattern across the row until 2 single crochet and the turning chain remain. Decrease 1 single crochet as you did in the beginning of the row and work your final stitch into the turning chain.

To decrease 1 half double crochet at each end of a row: Make 2 turning chains and skip the 1st half double crochet. Yarn round hook, insert into the next stitch and draw a loop through; insert hook into the next stitch and draw a loop through. This will give you 4 loops on the hook. Yarn round hook and draw through all the loops on the hook. Continue in pattern across the row until 2 half doubles and the turning chain remain. Decrease 1 half double as at the beginning of the row and work your final half double crochet into the turning chain.

To decrease 1 double crochet at each end of the row: Make 3 turning chains and skip 1st double crochet. Yarn round hook and insert hook into the next stitch and draw a loop through. Yarn round hook again and draw through 2 loops on hook. Yarn round hook again, insert hook into the next stitch, and draw a loop through. Yarn round hook and draw through 2 loops on the hook. There will be 3 loops remaining on the hook. Yarn round hook and draw through all the loops on the hook. Continue across the row in the pattern stitch until 2 double crochet and the turning chain remain. Decrease 1 double crochet as at the beginning of the row and work the final double crochet into the turning chain.

To decrease a stitch in the middle of a row: Work in your pattern until you reach the position of the decrease. Then, following the instructions that pertain

Decreasing one single crochet at each end of a row

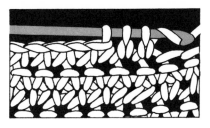

Decreasing one stitch in the middle of a row

Decreasing one half double crochet at each end of a row

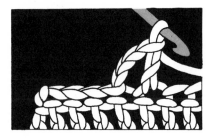

Decreasing several stitches at the beginning of a row

Decreasing one double crochet at each end of a row

to your stitch for decreasing at the beginning and end of the row, decrease 1 stitch over the next 2 stitches. Mark the position of the decrease with colored thread.

If your instructions require you to continue decreasing 1 stitch above the other, work the previously decreased and the next stitch together. The right side of your fabric will show the decrease slanting toward the left. Working the stitch before the previous decreased stitch together with the decreased stitch will show the decrease slanting toward the right. To keep a straight line of decrease, alternate the position of the decreased stitches: Work together the stitch before the decrease with the decreased stitch for one row; for the following row, work the decreased stitch with the stitch after the stitch decreased in the previous row.

To decrease several stitches at the beginning of a row: *Before* making your turning chain, slip stitch across the number of stitches to be decreased and into the next stitch. Then, crochet the required number of turning chains for your pattern stitch to form the first stitch, and continue in pattern.

To decrease several stitches at the end of a row: Work in pattern across the row until the required number of stitches to be decreased remains. Keep in mind that the turning chain of the previous row counts as one of the stitches. Simply turn the work in preparation for the next row, leaving the balance of the stitches unworked.

Increasing and decreasing in Afghan crochet

To increase 1 stitch at the beginning and at the end of a row: The increase at the beginning or left-hand side of your fabric is worked by inserting the hook into the horizontal loop that is between the first 2 vertical loops. The increase at the end or right-hand side of the fabric is worked the same way between the 3rd and 2nd loops from the end.

Increasing several stitches at left or beginning of a row in Afghan crochet

Increasing one stitch at the beginning and end of a row in Afghan crochet

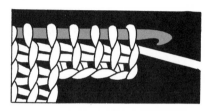

Increasing several stitches at right or end of a row in Afghan crochet

To increase several stitches at the beginning or left-hand side of a row: When you have completed the 2nd row of the pattern stitch, work the extra number of chains to give the necessary stitches, then go back along these chains from left to right picking up the working loops and continue in pattern into the main body of your work.

To increase several stitches at the end or right side of your work: Using a separate length of yarn, crochet the required number of chains and put aside temporarily. Work 1st row of pattern until you have reached the end of the row, then attach the separate length of chains by a slip stitch and continue working the basic stitch into each of the extra chains. Proceed with the 2nd row of the pattern stitch.

To increase 1 stitch in the middle of a row: Work the increasing stitch into the horizontal loop between the vertical loop at the required point of your fabric. If the increases are to be worked one above the other, then working into the previous increased stitch will form a line slanting to the left. Working into the stitch after the previous increased stitch will form a line slanting to the right.

To decrease 1 stitch at each end of a row: This is easily done by inserting the hook under the 2nd and 3rd vertical loops together and working the stitch as in pattern. At the end of the row work together the last 2 stitches before the final stitch.

To decrease more then 1 stitch at either end of the row: At the beginning of a row slip stitch over the required number of stitches to be decreased and just continue in pattern. At the end of the row simply leave the required number of stitches to be decreased unworked and begin working back to the left in the 2nd phase of the stitch.

To decrease 1 stitch in the middle of a row: Work as you would the decrease of 1 stitch at the beginning or end of a row. If the decreases are to be worked one above the other, mark the first decrease with a bit of colored thread. In the subsequent set of rows remember that working the stitch before the decreased stitch together with the previous decreased stitch will make the row slant toward the left. Working the previously decreased stitch with the next stitch will make the row slant toward the right.

Crab stitch edging

Edgings

One of the nice uses of crochet is as the edging of a garment. The basic fabric does not have to be crochet; crochet edging may be woven directly to knitted or to a loosely woven fabric. The edging does not necessarily have to be the same weight as the basic fabric. Be certain, however, that it is not too thick and clumsy or too skimpy.

Crab stitch edging. This is the simplest of all the edgings. It works quickly and gives a firm finish with the appearance of cording. With the right side of the fabric facing you, crochet 1 row of single crochet along the edge to be trimmed. Instead of turning the work, crochet another row of single crochet back along the 1st row already worked, *this time from right to left,* beginning by working into the last stitch of previous row.

Scallop edging

Scalloped edging. This edging looks best if worked in a contrasting color or even contrasting yarn. Be certain, however, that the yarn is about the same weight. Have the right side of the fabric facing you and work a row of single crochet along the edge to be trimmed. Turn, then work as follows: 1sc into the first st. * make 3ch, skip one st, sc into next st, rep from * to the end. Fasten off.

Shell edging. This will give you a deeper edging then the two previous samples; be sure, therefore, to take this into account when you crochet your fabric since it will affect the length of the finished piece. Have the right side of the fabric facing you and work a row

Shell edging

Picot edging

of single crochet along the edge to be trimmed. Turn, then work the shells as follows: 1ss into 1st st, * skip 2sts, 5dc into the next st, skip 2sts, 1ss into the next st, rep from * to the end. Fasten off.

Picot edging. This a dainty edging, ideal for fine yarns and often used for baby clothes. Work along the edge to be trimmed as follows: 1sc into each of the first 3sts; * make 4ch, then remove the hook from the last ch and insert it into the first of the 4ch, pick up the last of the 4ch, and draw it through the loop on the hook. This forms the picot. 1sc into the next 3sts; rep from * to the end. Fasten off.

Reversed ridge crochet (single)

Additional basic stitches

These simple variations of the basic crochet stitches are fun to know about and will give you some idea of the many ways that crochet stitches can be maneuvered.

Reverse ridged crochet. This variation is usable in any of the basic stitches, single crochet, half double crochet, or double crochet. Make the required number of chains plus the extra needed as a turning chain for your crochet stitch.

1st row Follow the basic instructions for any of the above stitches. Work to the end of the chain.

2nd row Crochet the necessary chains to count as the turning chain. Skip the first stitch and work the pattern stitch *into the back loop only* of each of the stitches in the previous row.

Eyelet double crochet   *Leaf stitch*

The 2nd row is your pattern row.

Eyelet double crochet. Make a chain divisible by 2, plus 1 chain and 2 extra turning chains.

1st row (RS) Into 4th ch from the hook work 1dc, work 1dc into each ch to the end.

2nd row 3 turning ch to count as first dc, skip first dc, 1dc into next dc, * 1ch, skip 1 dc, 1dc into next dc, rep from * to the end working last dc into 3rd of the first 3ch.

3rd row 3ch to count as first dc, skip first dc, * 1dc into 1ch of previous row, 1dc into next dc; rep from * to end, ending with 1dc into 1ch, 1dc into 3rd of the first 3ch.

The 2nd and 3rd rows form the pattern.

Leaf stitch. Make a number of chain stitches divisible by 2 and 1 extra turning chain.

1st row (RS) Into the 3rd ch from the hook work 2sc, * skip 1ch, work 2sc into the next ch, rep from * to last 2ch, skip 1ch, 1sc into the last ch.

2nd row 2 turning ch to count as first st, skip first sc, * work 2sc into next sc, skip 1sc, rep from * to the end. Finish with 1sc into the turning ch.

The 2nd row is your pattern.

Aran rib stitch

Aran crochet

Some crochet stitches have been devised to create fabrics that have the appearance of Aran patterns. The patterns can be built up row by row to give a three-dimensional effect as in Aran knitting, but it is much less complicated to work. Always use the traditional Aran yarn.

Aran rib stitch. This stitch is worked in the usual horizontal manner, and your pattern will emerge in the horizontal rather than the vertical. Make any number of chains to give you a practice square.

1st row (RS) Into the 3rd ch from the hook work 1sc, 1sc into each ch to the end. Turn.

2nd row 1 turning ch to count as first sc, skip first sc, * work 1sc into the horizontal loop below top loop of next st, rep from * ending with 1sc into turning chain.

Repeat the 2nd row several times and your pattern will be clear.

Aran moss stitch

Aran cluster in panels

Crochet moss stitch. Make a number of chains divisible by 2 plus 1 extra chain.

1st row (RS) Into 3rd ch from hook work 1 ss, * 1 hdc into next ch, 1 ss into next ch, rep from * to end. Turn.

2nd row 2 turning ch to count as first hdc, skip first ss, * 1 ss into next hdc, 1 hdc into next ss, rep from * to end. 1 ss into 2nd of the 2 turning ch. Turn.

The 2nd row forms the pattern.

Crochet clusters in panels. This pretty stitch takes practice but is well worth the effort once you have mastered the minor intricacy. Cast on 29 chains for your practice square. This will give you panels of 2 clusters and 4 double crochet between each panel.

Base row (RS) Into the 3rd ch from the hook work 1 sc, 1 sc into each ch to the end. Turn.

1st row 3 ch to count as first dc, skip first sc, 1 dc into each of the next 3 sc, * yrh, insert hook into next sc and draw loop through very loosely; rep this action into same st 3 additional times. You will have 9 loops on your hook. Yrh and draw through all 9 loops on hook. This may be called 1 Cl or cluster. 1 Cl into the next sc,

53

1dc into each of the next 4sc, rep from * to the end. Turn.

2nd row 1 turning ch to count as first sc, skip first dc, 1sc into each of the next 3dc, * work sc into the next st by inserting hook under the top loop of the first cluster made in the previous row, bringing hook back to the front around the small stem at the end of the first cluster, and completing the sc; rep the same st with the 2nd cluster. 1sc into each of next 4dc, rep from *. Work last sc into 3rd of the first 3ch. Turn.

3rd row 3ch to count as first dc, skip first sc, 1dc into each of the next 3sc, * 1Cl into each of the next 2sts, 1dc into each of next 4sc; rep from *; work last sc into first ch. Turn.

The 2nd and 3rd rows form the pattern.

Filet crochet

The word *filet* means "net," and the filet pattern is one of the simplest crochet patterns to work. It will produce a lacy fabric that may be put to numerous uses. Filet crochet consists of two basic stitches, the chain and double crochet. The spaces are formed by chains, and blocks of stitches are formed by double crochet stitches to correspond to the number of chains used in the open spaces.

Basic Filet net is formed by a single double crochet with a 2-chain space between each double crochet. Make a chain having multiples of 3 plus 5 extra chains. For example, 29ch.

Basic Filet

Blocks over spaces

1st row (RS)   Into 8th ch from the hook work 1dc; note that the 7 skipped ch form a 2-ch space on the lower edge. * 2ch, skip 2ch, 1dc into next ch, rep from * to end. Turn.

2nd row   5ch to count as first dc and 2-ch space, skip first dc and 2-ch space, 1dc into next dc, * 2ch, skip 2-ch space, 1dc into next dc, rep from * to end working last dc into 5th of the first 7ch. Turn.

The 2nd row forms the pattern. Each of the following rows ends with the working of the last dc into the 3rd of the first 5ch.

To work blocks over spaces: These are formed by working 1dc into the corresponding dc of the previous row, 1dc into each of the next 2ch and 1dc into the next dc. This forms a block of 4dc.

To work spaces over blocks: Work 1dc into the first dc of the block, 2ch, skip next 2dc and work 1dc into the last dc of the block.

Granny Square

Making granny squares

The simplest item to crochet is the granny square. It is achieved by chains, double crochet, plus joining with a slip stitch. It can serve a twofold purpose; you will learn about controlling your tension and it is a perfect way of using up odds and ends of yarn of the same thickness.

If you use a different color for each round, the new yarn must be joined at the beginning of each round. If you use one color throughout you avoid having to join the new yarn on every round.

Using one color: Make 6ch and join with a ss to the first chain, thus forming a circle.

1st rnd   3ch to count as first dc, 2dc into circle, 2ch, work * 3dc into circle, 2ch; rep from * twice more. Join with a ss into 3rd of first 3ch.

2nd rnd   2ch, work 3dc, 2ch, 3dc into first 2-ch space to form corner; * 1ch, work 3dc, 2ch, 3dc into next 2-ch space; rep from * twice more. Join with a ss to the first ch to first 2ch.

3rd rnd   3ch to count as first dc, work 2dc into first 1-ch space beyond ss of previous rnd; 1ch, * work 3dc, 2ch, 3dc, into 2-ch space; 1ch, 3dc, into 1-ch space, 1ch; rep from * twice more; 3dc, 2ch, 3dc into last 2-ch space, 1 ch. Join with ss into 3rd of first 3ch.

4th rnd   2ch, 3dc, into next 1-ch space, 1ch; * work 3dc, 2ch, 3dc into 2-ch space; 1ch, 3dc into next 1-ch space; 1ch, 3dc into next 1-ch space, 1ch; rep from * twice more; 3dc, 2ch, 3dc into last 2-ch space; 1ch, 3dc into last 1-ch space. Join with ss to first of first 2ch.

Break off yarn, draw end through loop on the hook and tighten to fasten off. Weave the 2 ends in on the wrong side. The squares can be made to any size depending on the thickness of your yarn and by working more or fewer rounds as you require. For additional rounds increase by 3dc and 1ch along each side of the square on every round.

Using two or more colors: Make the beginning ch and work first round as given for 1 color square. Break off yarn and fasten off.

2nd rnd   Join next color to any 2-ch space with a ss, 3ch to count as first dc; work 2dc into same ch space, * 1ch, work 3dc, 2ch, 3dc into next 2-ch space to form a corner, rep from * twice more; 1ch, 3dc into same 2-ch space as beg of rnd, 2ch. Join with ss to 3rd of first 3ch. Break off yarn and fasten off.

3rd rnd   Join next color in any 2-ch space with ss, 3ch to count as first dc, work 2dc into same 2-ch space; * 1ch, 3dc into next 1-ch space, 1ch, work 3dc, 2ch, 3dc into next 2-ch space, rep from * twice more; 1ch, 3dc into next 1-ch space, 1ch; 3dc into same 2-ch space as beg of rnd, 2ch. Join with ss to 3rd of first 3ch. Break off yarn and fasten off.

4th rnd   Join next color to any 2-ch space with ss, 3ch to count as first dc; work 2dc into same 2-ch space, * 1ch, 3dc into next 1-ch space; 1ch, 3dc into next 1-ch space; 1ch, 3dc, 2ch, 3dc into next 2-ch space, rep from * twice more; 1ch, 3dc into next 1-ch space; 1ch, 3dc

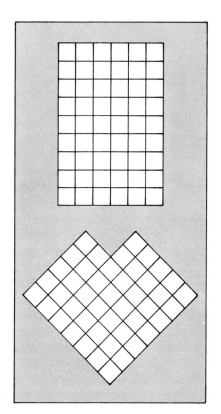

*Graph diagram
for designing
throw and poncho*

into next 1-ch space; 1ch, 3dc into same 2-ch space as beg of rnd, 2ch. Join with a ss to 3rd of the first 3ch. Break off yarn and fasten off. Weave all ends of the yarn where colors have been joined in on the wrong side of work. These squares also can be made in any size.

Granny squares can be put to many uses. The following design variations give you two simple ideas.

Plan your design scheme on graph paper as shown. This will give you ample opportunity to move your squares around for a more pleasing design or color combination. Then select the quality of yarn and hook size that will produce a texture that is pleasing to you. Work a square and measure the size exactly to see what the tension is. If it is either too small or too large you can change to a larger hook to increase the size or to a smaller hook to reduce the size. Or you can increase or decrease a round to achieve the correct size.

Poncho

To fit size 34/36 inch (86.5/91.5 cm) bust.
Length at center 28 inches (71 cm).

Poncho squares measure 4 inches (10 cm). Work 3 rounds only for each square. Make up 90 squares—45 front, 45 back. Press each square with a damp cloth and a moderately warm iron. Join 45 squares to form front as shown in diagram, do same for back. Then join shoulders.

The best method for joining squares is by single crochet. Use a yarn that is part of your color scheme. Using the same colors as you used for joining, proceed to work the finishing touches around the poncho.

Neck edging   With RS facing you work a round of sc around the neck opening.
2nd rnd   4ch to count as first dc and 1-ch space, skip 1sc, * 1dc into next sc, 1 ch; rep from * all around the neck. Join with ss to 3rd of first 4ch. Fasten off. Work 2 rnds of sc around the lower edge.

Afghan throw or rug

Work 4 rnds for each square in any color scheme you desire. Make up 54 squares. Press as for the poncho.

Join by single crochet using any color desired. Use the same color to work 2 rounds of single crochet around the edges. The addition of shell or scalloped edging makes a lovely final finish.

Blocking and pressing

Many yarns available today do not require pressing nor is it necessary with these yarns to block each section to the correct size. It is wise to check the yarn bands for precise details. The open textured weaves, however, do benefit with pinning into shape. Place each part right-side down on a heavy blanket or ironing pad. Pin evenly around the edge, making certain that nothing is stretched out of shape and that the stitches and rows are on a straight line. Check with your ruler or tape measure that your size corresponds with the instructions. Using a clean, damp cloth and a mildly warm iron, press evenly by placing the iron down and lifting it up without using the back-and-forth motion of regular ironing. Allow each piece to cool before removing from the pad.

Seaming

Crochet edges may be joined by stitching with a blunt-tipped tapestry needle using the same yarn as the piece was worked in. Depending on the finished article, you may prefer to use the single crochet method, which will give a firm edge without the ridge created by seaming.

Overcast seams With wrong sides facing you, match the two sections so that edges, rows, and stitches are in line. Pin, and check the right sides by opening the sections flat to see if all corresponds. Thread a blunt-tipped tapestry needle with yarn. Work two or more tiny stitches one on top of the other to secure yarn, * pass the needle over the top of the two edges from back to front, and pull yarn through. Repeat from * to end. Fasten off securely.

Single crochet seam Match sections as given for overcasting seams. Insert crochet hook from front to back through edge stitches of both pieces to be joined. Yrh and pull loop through, then complete one single crochet in the usual way. Continue with the single crochet stitch from left to right approximately ¼ inch (0.5 cm) apart until you reach the end. Fasten off. Using a tapestry needle, weave the small tail bits of yarn at the beginning and end of seaming into the seam itself.

This little book can by no means give all the information available regarding crochet. I hope it will lay the groundwork for the understanding of more complex books and patterns and bring pleasure to the left-handed crocheter.

I have enjoyed working on the left-handed books. I have learned a great deal and hopefully helped others to learn as well.

My thanks to everyone at the Victoria and Albert Museum for their patience and courtesy in helping me search through old records. My greatest thanks goes to Lucy Davis for her patient help and teaching.